CRACKLE OF ALMONDS

Gabriel Bradford Millar is a renegade American, born in New York in 1944. She survived five years of university in New York and Edinburgh, where she read with The Heretics, had poems in *Lines Review* and *Scottish International*, read her work on BBC TV, and was interviewed by George Bruce on BBC Radio Scotland. She married an Englishman and raised children and chickens in Gloucestershire, where she also taught A-level English at a Steiner school. Outposts published *Mid-Day* in 1977; then came *The Brook Runs* and *Bloom on the Stone*. *Thresholds – Near-Life Experiences* came out in 1995, and *The Saving Flame* in 2001. Gabriel has given scores of readings, sharing the stage several times with Kathleen Raine and George Trevelyan, and is noted for the incantatory power of her recitations from memory.

Gabriel Bradford Millar

CRACKLE OF ALMONDS

SELECTED POEMS

Darling Vivienne - after an amazing day to.gether - hope you share my love of Gabriel's poetry x x fine FitzGerald.

AWEN
Stroud

Published by Awen Publications 2012
78 Daisybank, Bisley Road, Stroud, GL5 1HG, England
www.awenpublications.co.uk

ISBN 978-1-906900-298

Production by Wordsmith Communication
Printed in England by Antony Rowe Ltd

No emblem of the realm,
I am the greylag goose,
the one that lingers,
that stays longer than
the other migratory birds

Acknowledgements

Previous publication of the following poems is acknowledged: 'Riding Light' in *Lines Review* (1969) and broadcast on BBC Radio Scotland (19 October 1969). 'The Inheritors (Sainte-Alvère)' and 'New Grief' in *Mid-Day* (Walton-on-Thames: Outposts, 1977). 'Two Straight Lines' in *New York Times* (1971). 'Sonnet', 'Credo', 'The Month of the Dead', 'Death Is a Soft Word', and 'The Wayfarer' in *The Bloom on the Stone* (Brookthorpe: Wynstones Press, 1978). 'A Note to Men' in *The Brook Runs* (Brookthorpe: Wynstones Press, 1980. 'Giga' in *Earth Ascending: An Anthology of Living Poetry*, ed. Jay Ramsay (Exeter: Stride, 1997). 'Deirdre', 'Before the Birth', 'The Fere', 'Lao Waking', 'For Akhmatova', 'She Scolds Herself', 'Hoi!', 'The Fool', 'For Beatrice', 'She Takes the Day', 'Fanny', 'A Sonnet', 'You Have Lain So Long (Song)', 'Crazy Lover', 'En Famille', 'We Will Not Say a Word', 'Be Horn', 'Thera', 'At Cock-Crow', 'Overheard at Ascot', 'Breathing Earth', 'Leda', 'Love Poem to My Husband', 'Menai Straits', 'To a Young Russian Poet and Lover', 'How Do We Go On?', and 'What Does a Man Really Want?' in *The Saving Flame* (Hereford: Five Seasons Press, 2001).

Contents

Foreword by Paul Matthews   xi
Manifesto   xiv

Grandmother   1
Hallowed on Broadway   2
For the Philosopher Simone Weil   2
This love no victim, never   4
Poet by Appointment to the Proletariat   4
Pater   5
Deirdre   6
Riding Light   7
Albino   8
The Inheritors (Sainte-Alvère)   9
Pitchcombe   12
Two Straight Lions   13
Overheard at Ascot   14
Before the Birth   15
The Fere   16
Sonnet   17
Credo   18
Jura Ferry Pier   19
A Note to Men   20
Lao Waking   21
The Hare (Song)   22
What shall my Magdalene do   23
The Month of the Dead   23
For Akhmatova   24
She Scolds Herself   25
Hoi!   26

Death Is a Soft Word	27
The Fool	28
In the Walled Garden	28
The Wayfarer	29
New Grief	30
For Beatrice	31
She Takes the Day	32
Dying	33
Fanny	34
A Sonnet	35
You Have Lain So Long (Song)	36
1982	37
Crazy Lover	38
The Yellow One	38
En Famille	39
Tidal Wave	39
They are not too beautiful	41
We Will Not Say a Word	41
Be Horn	42
For Thera	42
Thera	43
Giga	45
At Cock-Crow	46
Breathing Earth	47
Leda	48
Model with a Big Hat	49
Love Poem to My Husband	49
Menai Straits	51
What Does a Man Really Want?	52
The Muse	52
To a Young Russian Poet and Lover	53
How Do We Go On?	54
Today	56
On Patmos	57
You	58
Some Things	59

Manon	60
The Earth Speaks in Tunis	61
Come,	62
Where	63
Snob	64
Coherent	65
Duntisbourne Canto	66
Ancient Innocence	67
Venus	68
Man Says	69
In Exile Here	70
Anglo-Saxon	71
The Stone Says	72
New Gawain	72
Orkney Song	74
Facing It	74
Legal Brigand	75
Death Has a Majesty	76
I'll, Ill	77
What the I Says	78
Latest Word	79

Foreword

What Gabriel Bradford Millar has to say is that we need poetry. Sublimity. We die for want of it. 'Sub-lime' – I looked it up: it means the ability to reach up and touch the lintel. This poet has spent a lifetime doing that, thoroughly inhabiting the corner of the Milky Way that 'karma' (her word) has seen fit to grant her. Blake said the centre of the universe moves with us as we move. Well, Gabriel's elf-blood does make her feel in exile sometimes as she stands at the threshold, but she has vowed commitment to the guinea pigs, the husbands, the 'crackle of almonds in the pan' that each day brings, the 'bruises and sorrows' of the Gloucestershire town that is her dwelling place. 'This is where it happens.' Either the muse winks at us outside the fish shop, or, lacking eyes for the daily miracle, we languish in prosaic happenstance.

What stifles your song? This is Gabriel's constant question. What makes you turn away from who you most deeply are? ... Christ-man worthy of the ointment ... woman hemmed with gold. This New York citizen long resident in the Cotswolds is mostly content to quiz our quaint English behaviour ... 'Frightfully sorry to bother you, but I think your house is burning' ... a wry smile upon her face, but in no wise cynical. And yet. She is disconsolate at times, finding herself in a country 'where no tongue interprets what's in the heart'.

Read the book cover to cover and you meet a growing urgency. The poet's long devotion to familial things gathers power and scope until, 'plagued by the gravity of this sacred charge', she is authorised, free to speak without grandiloquence for the Earth: 'to praise her, / to state her case'. In the new poems that conclude this volume the 'rageousness' of Gabriel's concerns break through more blatantly. The house really is burning down, you know, and if the bankers who invest in landmines that blow off the legs of boys take no account of human interest in their ledgers then she must shrug off the veil of poetry a moment and use plain prose to say it straight.

Poets are responsible for the animals, one poet said, and here is a another who takes it seriously – magpie and ferret, the leaping hare, cock crowing the morning up, horse making 'epic use' of its muddy paddock. The way this poet proclaims their essential heraldic glory makes the more poignant her outrage in these last pages at the vivisector – not just misguided, she implies, but blasphemous of some inborn syllable within the creature.

Throughout the book Gabriel names her mentors. Kathleen Raine, Robert Bly, Anna Akhmatova, Simone Weil, Deirdre of Ireland, Norman MacCaig, Mary Magdalene, Christopher Smart, Sir Gawain are some of them – saints, philosophers, figures of high romance, but also poets in extremis of unfreedom or at the edge of sanity. These are tongues through which the heart does speak. They give her confidence. And in her need to hammer out a language for herself she turns (explicitly in a number of pieces) to the honest sweat of the Saxon smithies. Surprisingly, she makes no mention of her compatriot, Emily Dickinson. Yet the subtlety of the French and Latin that her poetry is also laced with – 'fripperies', 'prodigal', 'velocity', 'overture', 'insouciance' – convinces me she has schooled her ear in that most radical of academies. She knows with Emily that lost strata of the Earth are brought to light through delving among etymologies.

I am honoured that Gabriel names me among her accomplices. The first time I met her she assumed that we knew each other and had a work in words to do together. What work is that? To hold faith in magic in a literal age and keep the syntax limber. She has done her part in it. Poet that she is, she does not just write *about* the world; she dips her syllables in the bitter sweet of its 'gazpacho'. She thinks melodically. Does the Earth turn upon its axis? 'It turns on love.' This is the stance she assumes throughout – that word and world have an inside to them, that our lives are wound round with divinity, that love holds evidence enough for us to trust the endlessness of our biographies.

In our time of spellchecks and information technology such an unabashed romantic voice is rarely come by, and I am glad that it has found a publisher. It springs off the page – that generous tone uniquely hers which long ago took up residence in my ear. It has enlarged my faculties.

Paul Matthews

Manifesto

Poetry ought to be the most democratic of arts. We don't all play the cello or sculpt, but most of us in Britain can read and write, so the chance of a poem happening is theoretically quite high.

There was no place for poets in Plato's Republic – they were too subversive. In the thirteenth century the Inquisition condemned the Troubadours. And for seventy-three years the Soviet regime was suspicious of poets; writing poetry was often an anti-Soviet act punishable by imprisonment and hard labour.

Twentieth-century Anglo-American poetry, meanwhile, has focused on chronicling psychic and social collapse, starting with *The Wasteland* in 1922. But we get ill when we suppress the sublime. Buying into the collective dread in the world is another form of consumerism. Redemptive voices – such as Robert Bly, David Whyte, and Mary Oliver in America, Jay Ramsay, Paul Matthews, and Jehanne Mehta in England – lead us into a space of deeper perception beyond the reach of the five senses.

Rudolf Steiner prophesied that in our time more and more people would be reading, hearing, and writing poetry as a way of crossing the threshold between the inner and the outer. I see poetry as a matter of recognition: the listener recognises the poet's experience as something that resonates within them. I write to pay tribute to the innate savouriness of life. Grounds for love and delight abound. And for sorrow too, because we love.

Gabriel Bradford Millar

Grandmother

Don't think that because you are an old woman
You are entitled to your loneliness,
And your chintz peace where you sit secure from us
And miserable.

Don't you notice in your cup of afternoon tea
The bitter promise clotted at the bottom,
The durability of blood, beyond logic?

Forced at lovepoint out of your tidy immemorial room
In the lower Bronx, and brought to Connecticut
For the weekend, heaven ransomed, how you protest,
But not too much, the devotion of your daughter,
What you know to be guilty devotion.

Fold your hands, old woman, and abide.
The raised blue mole on your left wrist:
It is this the child sees when she looks at you,
This the child will remember.

Removed from youth twice, shouting in your silence
To the child beside you – in this blue mole you have
Your indelible being, and your unique life
We so worry over, and so closely ignore.

Old Greenwich, Connecticut, 1958

Hallowed on Broadway

It is necessary now,
when the months are passing
more swiftly than the year can follow,
that we do not depart from each other
in insouciance.
Syllables of explanation
languish on a tide of concern for you.

I would sit at the table
where you are master, serfless,
with affection for the direst dastard,
and share food with you that will give force
for a lovetime of living.

Instead we race here dying
in an embrace that keeps us apart ...
would that Juno were, my darling, gentle.

New York, 1962

For the Philosopher Simone Weil

A bruised plum squats on your plate,
    hurt beyond help.
Dreams are not round or logical,
    and health is a difficult thing.

At Le Puy you parried the timid and the vicious
(there is often no difference between them),
because you crossed the square to meet
an ouvrier, and sat down with him in a café,
        in the sun.
The middle class was your migraine, plaguing
        your brain and patience.
You were like the foundress of the Sacred Heart:
a day without suffering was intolerable to her.
But, in fact, you had no self-inflicted pleasures.

You were chronically waiting for God,
and all the time God was waiting for You.

In Marseilles you were welcome, and a worry –
you loitered in the portal, but would not come in.
        Tu étais exigeante.
Père Perrin loved you and was sad.
But doubt could not splinter you; the putty
of perhaps kept you intact.

In Spain a stout response brought you to a truth:
disgust with the rebels and the royalists alike.
From Kent you wrote to your parents as though
you were not dying, hiding it from them,
        magpie gay.

And all the while in the hospital refusing to eat.
The French Resistance troops were starving,
        you said, and you died.
Though hope disrupted the circle of your sleep.

New York, 1964

This love no victim, never

This love no victim, never,
of the merciless reign of time:

not founded on flesh,
on flesh it cannot founder.

This is no mortal love
murdered in a month.

New York, 1965

Poet by Appointment to the Proletariat

For Robert August Woodward, my great grandfather,
who took his own life at 26

The ice bends and thaws, but it was his intent
to move erect, unhampered by piety,
straightened by the threat of sham.

He would not fawn, he would not heel,
but marched with the marching man.
Self-sown, yeoman to no god.

There was dignity, too, in dying.

New York, 1966

Pater

When we arrived he was pushing the pram up and
down the room with the hagiography in his hand.
His hair and beard stood out in sizzled points like
escaped speech.
Domine, non sum dignus.

He could not get her to stop crying.
Verbalise it, baby, this is the expressive century.

Then he saw us.
Sit down. Have some wine.
He flung the book of saints in the pram and poured
the wine.
*Margaret will be back in a minute. I was just coaxing
the wee one into pastures rich and strange ... but I think
it's too soon after her nap. Some motortropism!*
he said, shaking the pram vigorously.

The baby stopped crying and stared at her father.
He grinned at her like a mad hermit.
She slept so long I was beginning to feel lonely.

He picked her up and they stared at each other nose
to nose. She focused on his spectacles, then on his
beard. He kissed her and she wrinkled up her nose.

*I don't like these long inarticulate silences when I
wonder what she's thinking. They make me nervous.
What are you thinking? You can tell me, I'm your
father. About the devaluation of the dollar? Psycho-
prophylaxis? Don't be shy ...*

He looked at us.
She's very close-mouthed with company.
He laid her back in the pram still staring at him.

Edinburgh, 1967

Deirdre

Argyll of the lag goose,
Argyll of the slow sky,
It was not for frolic
That the sons of Usna came,
And the foreboding glory
In the cloak of a woman,
Shyer than the hind,
Loner than the hare.

Theirs was Deirdre of the cool skin,
And the lochscape was a world
Of woman's shores
And woman's waters.
Always the path was strewn
With sweet devices.

Theirs was Deirdre of Ireland,
She of the long hair,
Born lovely to her cost,
She of the ermine-coloured skin.

Who comes on strong feet
To Deirdre of Etive,
Swift from the hunt?

With longing in his feet,
Swift from slaughter?

Not in these thousand years,
Not in Christendom,
Is one protected as she.
But *What is this doom?*

She murmured in her dream.
And the wind from the west
Whispered in her sleep:
The shadow of the wild ox,
The tooth of the wolf.

Edinburgh, 1967

Riding Light

for Norman MacCaig

Looking into the haggard face of the day
and seeing you, with your live intellect,
sparking across the cobble-brained city,
moving with humour and the care of
an affectionate father for his imperfect child –

I am reassured: fire eats damp air.
Your fiery mind is glowing in the rain.
I come to it for its original, grave laughter
in a gusty city, under a forsaking sun.

Edinburgh, 1969

Albino

The albino peacock from Australia
lifts an awful head, slowly, effetely,
to see if there is anything around that
he might be remotely interested in
being remotely interested in.

He takes his weird weight forward
on long spindles, like a dandy treading eggs,
and deceives us into thinking he is delicate –
he is merely decadent.

By some accident of taste he was made
so meticulous it sickens.
His eyes, precise in their perversion,
search the dirt for filaments.

The archetype in heaven who took snuff
and hid the fact, even from himself,
had a carved box to enshrine his habit.
Only the amateur is honest.

Toronto Zoo, 1969

The Inheritors
(Sainte-Alvère)

I

The silk shirt that I wear
Belonged to a man who climbed Mont Blanc
And crossed the Mediterranean in a canoe.
You say I am joking;
This time I am not.

In the evening the plum leaves
Are the colour of venous blood, unspilled.
High up the crimson plums
Look black at night.

After he died – who thought he would die,
With his old mother dying for years? –
How the old mother called for him;
Locked in her bed,
She rang out in the night,
A cracked bell.

We sleep in her death-bed
Between linen sheets.
With the ancient furniture,
Her dead son's face in a frame.

II

The wind brings the sound of the bell
From Sainte-Alvère, sonorous

Over the corn, keeping time
Where time does not care to be kept.

The sun mounts, a democrat, blessing
Indifferently. Poppies flare in the field
Like the last defiance before entering
The confessional.

Slowly the molecules of grapes turn
Water into wine. If it could be done,
I would revive the worthy man who
Lived in this house –

The day is too bright to miss.
They are all dead who lived here –
The mother, her son and her daughter.
Their cognac improves in the cupboard.

Gossiping with an old woman in the village
At the peak of the heat,
My eyes commute between her eye-beams
And her empty gums.

'Il était rigoleur
Tout l'aimait.'
'Mais il est mort, comme sa soeur,
De l'épuisement, en soignant de leur mère.'

Empress of his breath by blood-right,
She called for the chamber pot at night
And he brought it. A good son,
And he wasn't young.

And Germaine! Une femme d'un certain age.
Only a brother looked on your mellowing breasts,
Upon your undone hair.

Now the sun shoulders against the shutters
And the fifty acres are given back to God –
The house, farm, the other house and the woods
Greet another night.

It's clear what we are here to do:
We've brought a niece from England,
A distant cousin, as he died intestate.
We're to sort out everything
And try not to find the will,

In case he left it all to a secret paramour.
The old woman in the village knows –
'Sa mère l'ignorait. Elle ne supporterait
Ni liaison ni mariage.'

'Et l'amante?' I asked.
'Quand il est mort elle a pleuré, pleuré.'
She said she lived in that tower there,
But now she's gone away.

The niece is keen to get rid of everything –
The antiques, the linen and the lace ...
'Relatives' descend from Paris,
Carrying off the ivory.

An agent is greedy to help;
He's selling the whole estate –
A Paris banker is signing the papers.
Cicadas sing through the transfer.

III

Vines crawl like chains across the windows;
Tiles crack between their fittings.
Mould digests the trophies in the atelier.

The son, who'd made some bids for freedom,
Wrote in his diary the day before he died:
'Rien fait malgré le temps splendide!'

In the kitchen a young distant cousin
Flicks his hair out of his eyes and licks his lips.
Then he takes up a flute that he has found
And plays.

Sainte-Alvère, Dordogne, 1970

Pitchcombe

We have come through winter.
Take your cape off the hook;
comb out your winter hair
by the light of the long evening.

The season defects
in the silver light;
ice disappears.

We have come through winter.
Let me mark this fact with my
fingers on your face, and
pity the bird its claw.

Gloucestershire, 1971

Two Straight Lions

Two straight lions guard the gates of
      Babylon.
I have hung my heart in the gardens
      where
The cypress clings to itself, having no
      one else,
And oranges are still wild fruit.

Here eternity is a moment long and
      pleasures
Are monumental. In the morning
      Nebuchadnezzar
Splashes his pouched face with spring
      water,
Hoping for sun. On the hillsides rocks
      spout
Flowers, like leftover wine.

But remorse is unknown among men.
      We live
Before the conversion and the proof by
      fire.
The law is rage and harsh delight.
      The lion
Comes down hungry from the hill, while
      stars
Watch, weeping horribly.

It is only in the shadow of rocks and
      trees
That something like you, gentle,
      crouches,

Whose caught hind's eyes hold a
firmament
Where white dwarfs die.

Overheard at Ascot

– Excuse me, could you kindly remove your samurai from the small
of my back?

– My dear, you must come and see us! We're always in, except
weekdays and weekends

– Sorry to hear your wife died this morning ... never mind

– Not to worry, I always spill tomato soup on this white dress

– Frightfully sorry to bother you, but I think your house is burning.
It wants a note to the fire station ... I can give you their address

– My dear, it's mutton dressed up as lamb, but wear it by all means

(To host whose pet tiger is mauling his wife):
– I've nothing against tigers, as a rule

– Was that YOUR bullet that lodged in my brain? Of course you
must have it back; how thoughtless of me!

(Husband to wife's lover):
– Yes, could you return my wife ... I'd appreciate it awfully

Pitchcombe, 1971

14

Before the Birth

We live in the servants' quarters
of the Georgian house, where
two hundred years ago
on her first day,
the scullery maid
sat on her suitcase and
listened to her thudding heart.

We have three rooms facing south,
where the light of active heaven
rushes in on the kliegs of daybreak,
and the tits come hungry to the sill.

In bed, by the first light,
I put a hand on my belly,
on the miraculous mount.
Let me with the eyes of love
see the cosmic globe
downbraced and dreaming.

Nothing can undo this marvel,
not the ranting of
atheists or guns.

Pitchcombe, 1972

The Fere

(Old English – mate, companion)

Famed be	Your feorhus
for its	fairness,
for its	fine perfection.
If You stand	six feet
in sandals,	so tall
may we	one day stand.
When we have	worked and won,
when we	by white magic
turn sword	to psaltery,
when we	by white will-might
shift slaughter	to song.

Brookthorpe, 1974

16

Sonnet

Silence surrounds the moment when we meet,
And I am in the company of your soul
As though an opal, smooth and wholesome, turned
And the milk-light flowed to cordial blue.

Take your shoes off your feet –
In the ardent stillness now hold
Strong in the fiery marvel where we burned
Somewhere long ago, and now are new.

No surge of pleasures so persuasive as
This single silence that enshrines
A host of thrush songs and sonatas; and

No dance so grand, nor hug so magic as
This hope of godly kindness
Near extinct in the rush and bustle of the land.

Brookthorpe, 1975

17

Credo

The English word is a very life
And not a language only,
Breathing seasons, blowing seed
And fertilising snow.

Praise we the sea-brave Saxons
And their robust syllable,
For whom the foam was field and
Death an annex to the house of life.

The word moves down the hours,
Love in flood.
What fails and festers sinks to rest
And what is lovely goes above the grave.

Brookthorpe, 1975

18

Jura Ferry Pier

Some say here by this jetty
is the beginning,
this brute butt,
still as a witness at a birth,
the start where the rock
cradles the red water,
brutely silent,
before memory.

The cormorant keeps the span
of hungers and tides,
curling its neck
to the chronicle,
the squiggle on the rock.

And some say no,
here is the end,
where the cattle
came across in boats
and the drovers
drew each other's blood.
Where the cloud
comes down over Jura
like a shroud
on the shrilling gulls –
the end here
at the grey unspeaking rock,
at Rhuba Riabhag.

Keills, Kintyre, 1975

A Note to Men

Though you sit and smoke
until the stars go out,
though you sift philosophies
till you are baffled and dumb,
I am free:
I will never forget
the lute player's droopy moustache.

Brookthorpe, 1976

Lao Waking

Who comes in the snow-light,
Who comes in the morning?
Who sings at my side as the sun
climbs up over the hill?

A blue tit, a primrose,
a plaited polly –
gallant you come, gay-haired,
assuaging my sorrow.

As though no coercions had ever oppressed
the susceptible heart of man,
no slaughter, no madness,
no falling from God.

If I reive your loveliness,
claiming your lustre for my own,
it is part of a progress
towards consolation.

Who sees you remembers how ice melts
and every year elvers come,
finding the Severn,
from the Sargasso Sea.

Brookthorpe, 1976

The Hare
(Song)

Out on the moor see the boxing hare
Out on the moor in the morning
Early you will see him everywhere
Out on the moor in the morning

Keep a song in your bow
For the sun coming up
Keep a tune for the leaping hare

Round in a ring go the running hares
Round in a ring in the springtime
Some frolic in the middle, some are lying down
Some go round in a ring in the springtime

Keep a song in your bow
For the sun coming up
Keep a tune for the leaping hare

Prinknash Abbey, 1976

What shall my Magdalene do

What shall my Magdalene do
who longs for a Christ-man
to lavish her love on?
What shall she do with
this full jar of spikenard?

Brookthorpe, 1976

The Month of the Dead

The month of the dead
And the living rigid
At the onslaught of the cold.

And every year the same:
The soul is a battlefield,
The mighty powers in deadlock.

Every year it is different:
The rain is new dead speaking,
Weeping for our deafness,
Their tenderness streaming –
And we nearly hear.

While the magpie forages
In the field,
And the red ferret
Rifles below.

Brookthorpe, 1976

For Akhmatova

Far from the Neva, and the melancholy
of the old things going,
leagues from the grief of the one
who would not emigrate,
whose lids were at half-mast at
the perpetual funeral of romance
and the fast passing of innocence –

it is different here:
no snow after Easter.
The birds were muffled by the grave
at Komarovo.
Here the drama is domestic;
the heroine is celluloid and has a hero
who does not die for his truth,
or even live by it.
There is no knock in the night.

No, here the soul is purloined away slowly
by superpowers smiling like saviours.
The craven grab at pleasure has replaced
the noble joy of having backbone
and the lift of freedom.
For a mess of potage we have done
what Akhmatova would never do:
we have pawned our sacred essence,
we have sold our song.

Brookthorpe, 1976

She Scolds Herself

Happiness is like a holocaust:
you are never ready.
I see you,
hands on your ears,
turning back
from the terrible boom of love.

Brookthorpe, 1977

Hoi!

Though the days are short
and meant for work,
I have spent them rehearsing
the song I would sing to you.
But every time my fate
stopped me in the street
I looked away,
I pretended not to hear
above the beat of the traffic.

No more.
If the song crouches
too long unsung,
stars drop into graves,
pain prevails.

Hoi!
The sun to its work!
Here will stand one stalk
not cut at the bud;
here will lift one voice
above the prose of fear.

Life is wide:
there is room in it
for this small passion.

Brookthorpe, 1977

Death Is a Soft Word

Death is a soft word
For so radical a passage.
Is it to say the spirit
Is a tender thing in flight,
And only the manner of
Its release is gross, or,
As the papers say, disastrous?

Death, you are excellent
As the beauty of Emir;
You are a match for Emir
And would not love her only
For the flash and shudder.

Though you be cock's wattles,
Rageous as the sky at evening,
You are a new breath,
Failing none.
You are the last and best lover;
You never defect.

Brookthorpe, 1977

The Fool

The way he does it is this:
when he comes to a river
he takes a bridge
out of his pocket
and walks across

Brookthorpe, 1977

In the Walled Garden

You derive from lightning.
You are an angular radiance
and of use:
the vetch you like
locks nitrogen
into the ground.
Walled in, you speak
with apples and brassicas,
your will equal to the swelling work.

Oblivious of the ghosts
of the kingsmen who slept
with bloody hands in the hall
across the road,
you put your hopes
in an innocent row.

Some say the earth
turns on its axis –
it turns on love.

Brookthorpe, 1977

The Wayfarer

Thick the wind runs in gushes
Through the ditch,
And the clouds go doleful to the river.
I have set down my pack here
While the rooks caw in the ash tree,
Turning my back to the wind;
There the threads have not come unstitched.

There is no comfort in any country,
And least of all here,
Where all the amenities are observed.
No tongue interprets what is in the heart.
And I, meeting no one, have no call to smile.

The sky is true to its mood
And the birds do not dissemble.
In the wind I hear how fleeting is delight
And hope perplexed.

Since you passed away
I have thought of you, wife, once:
Last summer in the Sheepscombe valley
When a lark soared from her nest and sang
High over the yellowing corn.

Brookthorpe, 1977

New Grief

In spite of the fact that
This is the age of plain speech,
We are not candid with each other;
Our words, flung like stars,
Stick in a cold sky.

Wife of England, long-lived,
Comes with her shopping,
Trundles home with the tea
To a pre-fab in Pinner.
Closed shoots curl at her centre;
She has the serenity of the untried.

There is no pure unapologising passion
In the hearts of modern men,
No Blondel desperate for Richard
Across woods and highways,
But a new man, less sane,
Calling himself free.

Brookthorpe, 1977

For Beatrice

My friend,
why did you go back
to the more dramatic country?
There was a moon in our evening
and the little hills,
and the cornflowers
tall among the poppies.

You grew parsley
twangy as dragon's breath,
irony green.
You knelt on the ground
above the gradual leaves –
I loved the watch you kept,
and your Cherokee hair.

Confiding these seeds
to the earth now,
I pay tribute to you.
In Long Field
there are still bald ewes
and their bleating lambs.
And the wind!
Always the wind
whirring from the Severn.

Brookthorpe, 1978

She Takes the Day

A woman who is her own mistress
is the wind kneeling on a rock.
She goes to ground for discipline.
I know one who piles her black hair back –
but here is no Latin subjugation.
Her black eyes flash;
she is dangerous with enterprise.
She takes the day the way
a poet takes the page
and inscribes on the imbecile blankness
something lyrical and wild.

Brookthorpe, 1978

Dying

Sweet world, how you wrap your
already crowded arms around
a sick and fainting soul, pressing
to its notice, mercilessly,
the comforting paraphernalia of living:
a clock, a window, a pyjama top.
How sweetly existence recommends itself
to one who is about to leave it!

The room that limits,
the soldered, unopening corners
are the only cosmos that the heart requires,
having made its home and won
its special peace here.
Now it goes yet longs for
what it leaves behind, what
it loved so imperfectly and so little.
The dog in the fragrant manger
has a nose for blood.
Will you always hanker, heart,
after the unhuggable lover,
spending your brief beat in discontent?

Let go, let go, and after
the first astonished breath,
see what new air consoles your loss
and capers round you as around a guest.
See what hospitable host
hugs you at the door,
astounding your strongest hopes
with deathless welcome.

Brookthorpe, 1978

Fanny

You have chosen Spain
and the hermosa mountains,
wild rosemary and the arms
of a black-eyed painter,
darkness in the glare of the sun;
where the heart is tinder like the hills
the Basques set flare to in July.

You are the daughter of
the ambassador's man-secretary,
but you have to do with cobbles
and a ravenous cat.

You have chosen gazpacho,
the ancient recipe (said to have been)
given to Christ on the Cross –
tomato, cucumber, oil, garlic,
vinegar and bread.

We came into the Plaza Nueva
and waited for you,
and the sun scorched the edge
off our nervousness.
Then you came with your boy
down the cobbled steps
where the donkey clops
with the bags of bread,
down to the town where
everyone is a little mad, you said.

Lovely mother of Miguel –
who sees you in the Plaza Nueva
looks away changed,
his power awake.

Granada, 1978

A Sonnet

Soft in my hectic heart your voice,
A tenderly remembered friend,
Lifts up and bears me with it to the end
Of language and the edge of choice.

Then fast the light of day goes dark
And all its scrabbled matters fade;
Truth is of new dimensions made
And has a rich and different mark.

Silence is a subtle thread
Where vagrant talk is tethered like an ass.
But I would rather be to random wed,
Be speedwell bedding in the grass,
For all the footfalls on my head,
Than the rarest lily under glass.

Brookthorpe, 1979

You Have Lain So Long
(Song)

You have lain so long in my arms
I have your fragrance and your shape.
I am more now, and so are you.
Who made us knows how we move
in this strong communion:

I hold your hand and we glide
through the valleys of the dark ...
we drop words along the way
like bread crumbs,
so we can find the way back.

Brookthorpe, 1982

1982

Will we ever tire of tenderness?
Will the angels yawn?
The energy of tenderness makes
a tabernacle of the ticking clock;
the moment gleams deathless
in the amethyst.

Eternity utters it in a wing tip,
in the tree's green ouverture.
The mare's joy and the church bell
declare it,
the soft hullabaloo of the lamb
at its milk.
We grow landwide admiring this.

Will we tire of miracle?
Does God stop breathing through us
when we forget Him?

Lions proclaim the sun glows;
they do not prevaricate
nor lose the scent of the gold.
Does the spirit live?
Goat's hair and oil say so.
Eternity answers, squeezing
into the hour's empty sepulchre.

Brookthorpe, 1982

Crazy Lover

God is a crazy lover –
He nailed Himself on a tree
For love of thee, fair lady,
All for love of thee.

Brookthorpe, 1983

The Yellow One

Our younger girl, the yellow one,
reminds me of the melon in the market:
far from its origin it looks domestic.
She knows where her sister has left her shoes.

The night we heard that a friend had died
and I couldn't eat any supper,
she got down from her chair and held me
while I cried.

She has made a diet sheet for her guinea pig.
She says writing poetry is a waste of paper.

Brookthorpe, 1983

En Famille

The pathos of waking up together again,
and not acknowledging it, again,
lunging out of the house into mild rain –
makes an ache like the death of one
taken for granted and loved too late.

If there were an earthquake instead,
instead of bread on the plate,
and the house fell in just as
I was plaiting your yellow hair,

I would dig like a dog,
unstoppable,
I would dig like a dog in the rubble
for a bone I knew was there.

Brookthorpe, 1984

Tidal Wave

'E tardi!'
Violetta cries –
Germont's change of heart …
too late.
And so it is.
Too late to warn the bathers.

Indifferent as a thief,
the tide runs off with lives
like loaves of bread,
like coins
more wonderful than gold.
Not one will be minted
like that again.

You could say
the first world,
the overfed creditor,
sends food with all
the velocity of guilt.

You could say
the furled fury of the wave
was a reply to
the uprooting of the mangroves
or the civil strife on Sumatra.

Its ghastly charisma
now features at the cinema
of our global psyche.

What is there to say
that has more dignity
than silence?

Brookthorpe, 1987

They are not too beautiful

They are not too beautiful,
these women of the west,
not like the women of India.
They go out into
the unholy multiplicity
with no gold thread
in their garments.

What do they bow before?
It is hard to know.
Sometimes their love
is all for their dogs.

Brookthorpe, 1986

We Will Not Say a Word

We will not say a word about love
That is so overspoken,
Nor tax each other with declarations
Trumped up out of tradition
For want of the real word.
The heart is a rich king,
But the tongue, his servant, is very poor.
It is enough to know
You are awake somewhere,
Sharing the gravity of the earth
With me now,
The struggles and trumps
Of the century.

Brookthorpe, 1988

Be Horn

Be horn of plenty, heart,
Be skyey, never counting costs;
Be prodigal as rain, and brave.

For the law is this:
The more love let out of the horn,
The more tumbles out behind.

Though we lose the way
And dark clasps us –

How warm the breath still,
How the pain shines.

Hawkwood, 1989

For Thera

I would conjure for her
the great Egyptian fire,
to make her soul
a strong alloy –
Hathor!
an hour of your heroic joy!

Amberley, 1989

Thera

(Ancient Greek – wild, beautiful)

She fumes, she smoulders,
an undetonated Etna.
I have learned to tiptoe
round the edge of her –
if I come too close she'll blow,
or run, God knows where …

But I love her,
even when she's looking.
I offer her food;
I give her money, comfort,
medicine.
I love the one she has not yet
discovered in herself.

She has a classic Latin face;
she could be Italian or Greek.
At school she drew the head
of a Renaissance prince
who had her great sad eyes.

Her father named her for
the island in the Aegean;
the Therans were the ferrymen
between Mycenae and Egypt.
But when the volcano blew
it threw up a wall of water ninety feet
that dashed to Crete in half an hour,
seventy miles away. The suckback
took the houses into the sea –
Crete went extinct.

On Thera they got away in boats.
All but a pink pig perfectly preserved
in the volcanic ash.

Yes, I love the dark, the latent daughter,
sure that one day she will savour
her distinct space and time,
finding a new use for fire,
warming the world with it
where she goes.

Amberley, 1989

Giga

Gay mare, dancer,
frankly female:
I applaud your caper
in the jeopardy of space,

the frank caprice of the
female without a foal.
Agape, I watch you
trample the status quo.

White, wiry,
freckled and erotic,
your kicking heels are
incontestable as time.

Your flank includes
the first delight of things
when they first found
that they could fly.

Alive, with no apology,
you find an epic use
for the muddy paddock –
the very genesis of joy.

Amberley, 1990

45

At Cock-Crow

At cock-crow the gouging fist of light
floods the stage and the masque resumes.
Glamorous the disguise, and eloquent,
where we are veiled from ourselves.

Love rends the veil
and reveals the beat of the heart,
undissembling as birds in the lilac
in the lunging rain.

Love of miles, love of hours,
Love of portals and starts.

Pale the heroes of Matterhorn:
I toss my hat for him
who has lived through the day
without bluff.

Amberley, 1990

Breathing Earth

Am I ready
to greet the breathing earth?
She's ready.
Past ready.

How shall I reply
to the passionate planet –
vermillion in the west
and the hill brooding indigo;

green ground in the morning,
generous and strong,
rosebay willow herb,
fat apples and mallow?

I am plagued by the gravity
of this sacred charge
to praise her,
to state her case.

Amberley, 1991

Leda

Her mother waited at home while
she went down to the river, but
this morning for Leda it was not the same:

she felt sharp, she felt danger.
She started to sing as she always sang,
but she heard her voice poised

on the edge of knowledge.
Her blood was alert, as it would be later
when she laboured to bring forth stars.

And there he was, curving with the river,
intent on her. How terrible to be
singled out, for salvation or slaughter.

She protested,
thought once of home, and
hoped the imperious swan would win.

Harescombe, 1992

Model with a Big Hat

by Vuillard

There you are, Vuillard,
come from your mother's house,
your sober celebrity chez les Nabis
like a badge you wear under your coat.

But the model with the big hat –
it will fall off if you hug her –
she will not be shy and ashamed.
She will show the crooked front tooth
that will besot her lover.

And you will translate her into paint,
intimate but monastic man.
You cannot say it outright,
but your allusions to ecstasy will lurk
in the vermilion breast, the cheek.

Stroud, 1993

Love Poem to My Husband

Prince manqué,
I will come with you,
though your palace is blasted
by the cannons of time,
and your servants are all free
with a terrible freedom.

49

You still walk like a prince
though your horse has galloped off
to the valhalla
where noble horses go.

You don't offer comfort;
you give provocative advice.
You assume that the other, like you,
is in training for a higher mission
with a secret agenda he has not yet seen.

I am not your way through,
but I will go with you
through the deserts of the soul,
the weeks of ennui
when the only distraction
is the hoofprints of strange camels.

I will go with you into
the thronged and monotonous markets
that make us forget why we've come,
and the funerals of our friends where
we remember that we have not yet done
what we came to do.

I will go with you while we learn this:
no matter what –
after every odyssey a port,
after every death an easter.

Stroud, 1995

50

Menai Straits

Anglesey

We talked to the man at Penmon
who told us how deep the straits were,
how treacherous the current, fast.

But we had been wrecked
that week already,
and we knew:
it is we ourselves who betray us,
not the depths of the Menai,
not the swift tide.

Stroud, 1997

51

What Does a Man Really Want?

If they had asked Gawain
What does a man really want?
would he have said
A man wants to cut virgin timber,
or A man wants a hoyden in bed?

I say, in his sanctum, A man wants
a goddess of joy,
he wants Hathor, the Great One,
who knows what he wants
and will love him no matter what.

No hoyden, Hathor,
and no maiden either –
she lives as an incandescence
in his soul,
and he longs for this,
whether he knows it or not.

Stroud, 1998

The Muse

The muse will wink at you anywhere –
in the High Street,
at the dead fish stall …
she may come on spiked heels
in a tight skirt and wink.
If you miss it,
you will have to live
through a long prosaic day.

Stroud, 1999

To a Young Russian Poet and Lover

If we met now,
thirty years from New York,
countries away from our youth,
would I know your face?
Would it be crinkled with love
or ravined by lack of it?

Would I know your eyes
and the smouldering melancholy
of your soul in them,
the plunging hunger of your Russian soul?

Torches your eyes, they started fires,
first with my tinder –
we were seventeen
and it burned till twenty.

God, I loved you –
on Broadway,
out all night in the park.
I loved you in lecture halls.

We lived on kisses,
on myths, ciphers and music:
Bessie Smith and Jelly Roll,
Shostakovich and Ives.

Let me say that
young love does not die –
it goes underground
and fertilises the rest.

'If we should some day move apart,
we still will have the song.'
That's what you wrote in
'The First Snow of Winter'.

And if we met now
I wouldn't want to hear
how many degrees you have, or cars,
but whether you danced
to your heart's song
or stifled it.
That's all.

Stroud, 2000

How Do We Go On?

for Christopher Smart

How do we go on
when our blood has forgotten the glory?
The broken bird limps in the dusk,
his wings gone, and his song.

Different now from the time
we played by the wide Nile,
or stood on the edge of the Negev …
or ferried Greeks across
and the dolphins delivered us.

Where now is the Chartres blue
that regaled us,

the plainsong, the passion,
the joint thrust
that punctured the sky?

The new man is an old goofer
gaga with amnesia,
distracted by trifles,
who has sold his birthright
for a quick buck.

And Christopher Smart,
you warned us with your life.
Unhinged, your door
no longer swung smoothly ...
how could it after what it had done:

admitted you to the mystery
and you could not stand the dazzle,
you were undone?
Your second language was Angelic
in your jubilant brain.

Upper Grange, 2001

55

Today

My mouth splits like a gourd;
seeds of gratitude spill out.
This is different from
delight in the white rose
or the sunny ardour
of blown woad, or
the deep feast in
the sweetness of beeswax.

Today I am blown over:
both my daughters are fertile
at the same time,
one starting as the other ends.
My man is finding silence
in the Austrian alps.
They are all on track,
on the Wanderweg,
winding through
the inner hinterland.

And I,
I am the centurion who fainted
at the empty tomb,
the centurion when he came to,
and all the days of his life
after that.

Upper Grange, 2002

On Patmos

On Patmos, in the hamlet
on the brow of the hill
she was there –
the old woman in black
in the courtyard
under the arbour,
sweeping the leaves
that the sea wind
had wrested from the vine.

A little white house
with blue windows
on its fraction of paradise ...
prolific fat figs
and garlic in rows,
potatoes,
a geranium alarming
against the whitewash,
a jack-in-the-box.

We stood on the road
and watched her.
She looked up,
stopped sweeping
and smiled,
toothless and seraphic,
at peace
under the generous sky.

Upper Grange, 2003

You

You from Montreal, I from New York –
we have found our place in the rain.
Literal and lyrical, for twenty springs,
our days have been taxed and graced.
We have paid bills and sung carols
in inimitable England.

Now you stand here in a silk shirt
and an indigo hat from Mad Hatter –
we are going to supper with a friend.
And I think:
I must remember you like this
against the time when you walk
into another realm,
where there is no rain,
no silk shirt, no hat.

Stroud, 2004

Some Things

Some things I cannot leave behind:
children, husband, friends;
the smell of pine on the steep path
in the Schwartzwald,
where we met the old holzhacker
fixing the crucifix,
the bench by the chapel at the top
where the sun grinned down.

Salmon and garlic and sweet potatoes,
the crackle of almonds in the pan.

I am not an extinctionist,
I'm a fan of karma and reincarnation.
But how can I leave all this?

I will abscond with the priceless cameos
and extol all these things in heaven.
Death will not put its hand over my mouth.

Stroud, 2007

Manon

Modigliani doe
from the Vosges –
Jerome must miss you
in Colmar.
You are made
for balmy nights
when the oiseau-mouche
smooches with the flower
in the garden
of the auberge.
Where, above, the wild boar
roots for truffles.

But you are here
scrubbing beetroot
in a clinic,
where the air is
wavering with rain,
far from summer
and your man.

Almond-eyed,
long-throated doe –
go home soon.

Park Attwood, 2007

The Earth Speaks in Tunis

'I love you so much,' she said,
'I will use every element to tell you.'

So the gold wind of the sirocco
swirls in the street,
into nostrils and doorways.

The wild hair of the wind
wraps around lamps and palm trees,
twining with the night-black hair
of the women.

North, by the sea, Sidi Bou Said,
proud of its palace,
dreams of the fez.

And Carthage, its cousin,
keeps watch in the graveyard.
In its lap sleep Phoenicians and Greeks.

A young woman from England
lies roasting on the ruins
with a fever of 107,

delirious
in armoured company
and a babble of old tongues.

'South of Tunis, in the desert,
the library of stones holds
the memory of aeons:

catalogues of ravages,
floods of love surging
from the souls of saints –

the stately parade of epochs
peoples your sleep.
I am awake while

you sleep, my children,
you sleep through your life
while I work.

In a dumb dense sleep
you are merciless to your brothers …
that breaks my heart.

The number of times
my heart breaks
must baffle the abacus.'

Stroud, 2008

Come,

Come, let us eat together
and stave off the hour of death.
Now, while you are telling us
what self-consciousness means to you,
we are all a little more alive.
Something is lit
that only company can kindle.

Stroud, 2010

Where

for everyone who'd like to give voice to his or her soul through an artistic medium

Where does it come from,
the Olympic longing
for the company of an angel,
this furious impulse
to console the lonely,
to let the birds out of their cages?

Where is the place for this potency
where the prosaic cannot go?

I want to be a keeper
of the pictures of power.
When I had children
I banished the daimon –
he was too dangerous.
But I tell you:
the daimon gets angry
when he is ignored.

Attend to your daimon, friend –
Attend, attend.

Stroud, 2010

Snob

Lost in the dogleg lanes of the brain,
like the chartless wilds of New Zealand …
let me be illiterate and sweet,
a worker in beeswax,
a candle maker.
Not this quibbling snob
that pokes at the mote
in everyone else's eye.

Dunedin, 2010

Coherent

I'd like to be coherent
like the number one,
a single integer
with integrity.

Like a gannet,
with one thing in mind.
Or a grand dame I know
(one hundred),
afloat on her philosophy:
'It's all very interesting,
I'm so grateful for everything.'
The august one,
with a surplus of patrician leisure
and the gumption to live it.

But no, my brain
is a jumble sale,
a great-gapped colander
through whose plural holes
slips my life's purpose,
split into pleasures
and the long postponement,
as though the body
were itself immortal.

Stroud, 2010

Duntisbourne Canto

We came to the Saxon church of St Michael,
who is always happiest on high ground.
By the altar wall overlooking the wood,
we sat in the lap of magisterial calm.

We sat with the Shaper of grass and silence,
Lover of life and her brother, death.
Charmed by the lark we called 'the fugitive divine',
we forgot that it is we who always flee.

Here time had no truck with us,
and Hester Boulton in her tomb
had long ago stopped looking
at the kitchen clock.

It was a cool womb we went into
through the age-worn door.
And there we knew: the dark oak pews,
heavy with reverence, great with longing,

will never be delivered
of their worthy burden,
nunc et semper,
world without end. Amen.

Stroud, 2010

Ancient Innocence

The sweet interstice between your eye and cheek –
I admire this as you read *The Secret Stream*,
a book about Rosicrucianism.
You don't trust newspapers,
but you trust this news.
Your thinking is subtler than your speech –
it is the green that Gwen John made
from chrome yellow and black,
innocent and ancient, surprising and wise.

No muscle is malicious,
no muscle angry,
there is no gossip with you,
no slumming along the floor
of the astral.
I do that for both of us.
I rage against the liars –
the warmongers and the vaccinators;
I write to them.

And come back to you for mystery,
and relief from the trap of matter.

Stroud, 2010

Venus

J'attends pour les hommes qui me vainqueront,
et je ne serai pas vaincue en un jour.
Je ne serais pas vaincue par les faibles,
ni les hypocrites ni les médiocres.
Mais par les hommes ayant du courage
comme les Vikings, comme les enfants.

Envoyez-moi les meilleurs du pays;
prêtez-moi les hommes élus.
Ceux-là, je les embrasserai;
ceux-là, je les appellerai mes maîtres;
je les appellerai mes amants.

*

I am waiting for the ones who will conquer me,
and I will not be conquered in a day.
I will not be vanquished by the feeble,
by hypocrites or the tepid.
But by men with courage
like the Vikings, like children.

Send me the bravest of the land;
lend me the elect of your men.
These I will embrace;
these I will call my masters;
these will be my lovers.

Stroud, 2010

Man Says

I live, therefore I suffer.
The squirrel does not yearn
for a string quartet,
or feel it is living
below its potential.

The dog does not long to do good,
to teach English to Slovenes
or save orphans from loneliness
in their cots.

Only man knows:
I live so I suffer,
my life is too small
for my soul.

Where is everyone?
What are they doing?
Tonight it is not alright
to be alone.

Stroud, 2011

In Exile Here

Where women bark at their children,
on this planet of spilled blood and sorrow,
I am on red alert – angry at the banks
and the makers of landmines,
livid with governments that
hold us in the thrall of terror
to justify a military mania.

Sick of wars that break Nature's heart
and hatred that makes her heave.
Ask anyone – love is always
harder to bear than death.

But I made a vow to come back here,
to the place of bruises and sorrow.
We are not here to die an early romantic death;
we are here to serve.

Listen – someone's coming …
Is the candle lit by the door?

Stroud, 2011

Anglo-Saxon

Give us the sweaty speech
of the Angles and Saxons –
whaling, warring, drinking and singing,
the boast of the board,
goblets clonking on oak.
No 'concatenation' or 'judiciousness' –
they don't scan.
Not the pale face and blanched hair
of the barrister,
the Latinate lingo and anaemic talk.

Bring on the rowdy dong
of 'modgedonc' –
honest Saxon syllables –
Let's have them.

Stroud, 2011

The Stone Says

In Kabul I didn't want to hurt the girl –
I was helpless in the hard man's hand.

I am the hidden backrest of the earth;
I will support her till I smelt in the sun.

Build your holy circle
and your house with me –

Brendan built a jolly one in Dingle
with stones like elephant feet.

But don't throw me at anyone,
please –

I was never meant
to take the place of your heart.

Stroud, 2011

New Gawain

Gawain at my table,
hamstrung in battle,
declines wine,
declines whisky.

Once in Scotland
someone said,
'Poetry is incapable of
dealing with the complexities
of modern life.'

He stood up,
swung his sword-tongue
and silenced the foe.

'Poetry is always capable
of dealing with the complexities
of the heart,' he said.
'That's what it's for.'

The knight got up early.
The sun over Stroud
saw him mount,
avid for the road.

He left an aroma of vanilla
on the pillowcase,
the scent of a saint or a baby,
though he is neither of these.

Gawain at my table,
hamstrung in battle –
with time the snapped hamstring
will heal.

Stroud, 2011

Orkney Song

Silkie, sweet silkie,
If thou wilt be mine,
I'll give thee a bothie
And twelve head of kine

I'll make thee a fire,
A fine gown of wool,
That thou may forget
Thy deep kingdom so cool.

Stroud, 2011

Facing It

This is the place.
This is where it happens;
not in Spain,
not in Mas de St Jerome –
that was the Spenders'.

Right here,
in the oldest road in Stroud,
in this sliver of a house,
piled with the paraphernalia
of a life:
papers, bars of soap, a cat.
This is the place.

The Studio, Stroud, 2011

Legal Brigand

The High Street bank,
the daylight bandit,
claims to give interest,
but the disinterest in us is insulting:
inflated lending rates and tuppence
for the use of our money.
Legalised piracy
in a respectable setting.

The pirate in a suit is suave.
He sits at a desk and says,
'You can only borrow money
for home improvements.'
'I need £4,000 to pay debts.'
'I'm sorry, that's the rule.'
This is called customer service.

On the questionnaire the bank,
vivisector of cats,
patron of landmines
that blow off boys' legs, asks,
'Are the premises clean?
Are the staff polite?'

'Yes, yes,
it's what you do with our money
that is so offensive.

A wolverine,
ransacking a cabin in Canada,
has more integrity.'

Stroud, 2011

Death Has a Majesty

Death has a majesty I, live, will never know.
Tawdry beside it, I become a prole.
The long breath going out took you with it.
Free of the fripperies of a life,
you lie in state in the window bay
by the birches, and you almost smile,
like Lakshmi in the land you loved.
You had a talent for gratitude
and you look grateful for this too.

Death has a streamline that I, checked, have not.
Motley beside it, I stand cap in hand
before the lustre of your soul –
the white, white gold.

Stroud, 2011

I'll, Ill

It's good to be acute and boiling,
like knickers in a zinc tub;
good to have to stay still
and watch the apples fatten.

The flavours of a life rise up,
pictures in the story that console us
for having to be born.

The old word 'consolatio' –
the monks in the Middle Ages knew …
if her eyes were speedwell and her hair
a cornfield in the August sun,
they would have to forgo
this consolatio.

Now the bubbles from the tub
are past love times and magicks –
the white hair of my father,
his mellow voice,
my mother in the garden.

Then New York and cherry pie
with a lover in Riverside Park.
A cottage in England and children
running in from the field …
the cinema of memory
with a cast of thousands.

If we do not let our lives delight us,
what hope is there for the world?

Stroud, 2011

What the I Says

I have come again through fire.
Through the imperative of levity
I have been in intimate
and majestic realms.

And now, through the thrust of mercy,
another chance,
and the gallant hand of gravity,
I am back.

I remember Egypt
and the inside columns,
and Greece where the temple
was the body of the god.

I am the bull,
the lion,
the eagle
and the man.

Hear this:
there is nothing
I do not survive.

There is nothing
I do not survive.

Stroud, 2011

Latest Word

The passion of dawn be with you,
the blaze of dusk;
a heart with a swan's faith,
a firm hand at the wood.

I am lighting the flame for you
and cooking the salmon.
The Lord of Time be with you
in your going and coming –
now until the world's end,
now until then.

Stroud, 2011

List of Subscribers

Anahita Aghili
Nicholas Allan
Peter Allan
Matthew Barton
Naomi Brandel
Richard Brinton
Daniela Code
Kate Collier
Helen Cranston
Sabine Crittall
Mathieu Demers-King
Alan Dring
Mike and Rosemary Duxbury
Marion Fawlk
Prue Fitzgerald
Andrew Floyd
Jasmine Frances-Hawksley
Valerie Gillies
Elsie Hatton-King
Alexandra Howard
Polly Howell
Bernard and Karin Jarman
Geraldine Lander
Judith Large

Katie Lloyd-Nunn
Kevan Manwaring
Clare Marsh
Frances Marsh
Jehanne Mehta
Jobo Mehta
Stephanie Margaret Melliar Smith
Anthony Nanson
Nick Naydler
Mrs L. Oldfield
Jennie Powell
Jay Ramsay
Maxine Relton
Yvan Rioux
Alan Rycroft
Paul Sander-Jackson
Matthew Sell
David Shaver
Peter Stephenson
Michael Steward
Jackie Stoff
Greg Tricker
Daena Turner
Antonia T. West